PRIDE

Coloring Book

Inspiring Designs with Affirming Messages of Love and Acceptance

by

Ronald Holt and

William Huggett

Cover Design: pro_ebookcovers

Editing: Spencer Hamilton, the Nerdy Wordsmith

Author photos: Michael Gomez, www.GomezPhotography.com

Thank you for selecting this coloring book, which is a companion book to PRIDE: You Can't Heal If You're Hiding From Yourself. To thank you for purchasing this book, we'd like to offer you a free downloadable pdf version. Go to www.DrRonHolt.info to sign up. We hope you find the content helpful, whether you identify as a LGBT person, family member, ally, or someone who is simply open to messages of hope, inspiration, and healing. As you go through this book, you may engage in whatever feels most meaningful to you; however, many people have found the act of coloring to be helpful as a form of meditation, and we invite you to try this if it resonates with you.

When working with clients who are starting a meditation practice, we often use breathing as a focal point. In this form of meditation, breathing is used as a place to return to when the mind wanders. As thoughts and feelings occur, we simply notice them, acknowledge whatever comes up, and then gently return the attention to the breathing. Over and over again, the mind will venture off to a thought or feeling. Each time it does, we simply become aware of this and bring the attention back to the breathing.

If you use coloring as a method of meditation, you may want to try using the mandala as your focal point. Notice whenever your mind wanders off, then gently bring your attention back to the focal point of the mandala. We've included various quotes, inspirational messages, and affirmations in this book. If you like, you can use these as starting points for your contemplation and meditation.

One of the themes in the book is that unity, strength, and healing come when we embrace our diversity. Mandala is a Sanskrit word that means "circle" or "sacred circle." A circle can also remind us of infinite unity because it has no real beginning or ending. It is a continuous flow. Each point flows into the next point and forms a cohesive whole. Likewise, each one of us is part of a cohesive whole that is the circle of life. Sometimes we focus more on our differences and lose contact with the unity of our shared humanity.

All of humanity benefits whenever a single individual's life is expanded. So as you go into the stillness of coloring, we encourage you to enter into whatever process allows your deeper self to emerge. We invite you to grow and expand into the beautiful, authentic person that only you can be.

Sincerely,

Ron and Bill

"You can't cross the sea merely by standing and staring at the water."
–Rabindranath Tagore

You are here today, reading these words, contemplating the mandala. Take this opportunity to go inside yourself.

Even though there are many things you cannot control, you must journey forward. Trust that you will get to where you need to go. Set sail. Trust your deeper self to guide you.

Affirmation: Today I will start my journey.

> **"You yourself,**
> **as much as anybody in the entire universe,**
> **deserve your love and affection."**
> **–Buddha**

Even though it may not be safe to be out to others, it is important to be out to yourself. When you remain hidden from yourself, you are in effect saying, "I am not worthy of being acknowledged."

However, when you come out to yourself, you reverse that message. When you acknowledge who you are, you now proclaim, "I AM worthy". This message will filter down to the depths of your being and you will create space in your life for deeper healing.

Honor yourself today and every day going forward.

Affirmation: I am worthy and I fully accept myself.

"There are all kinds of love in this world, but never the same love twice."
—F. Scott Fitzgerald, *The Short Stories of F. Scott Fitzgerald*

You are unique. Allow yourself to fully embrace all of who you are and become aware of all the ways that you love. No one else can determine who you love or how you love. Your love is yours to give, so give it away freely and generously.

Affirmation: Today I commit to loving in the many ways that are unique to me.

"Your time is limited, so don't waste it living someone else's life. Don't be trapped by dogma--which is living with the results of other people's thinking. Don't let the noise of others' opinions drown out your own inner voice. And most important, have the courage to follow your heart and intuition."
–Steve Jobs

You have been given a most precious gift--human life. But this gift of life is a time-limited gift. Life is short and it is too precious to waste even one moment living according to someone else's expectations. Use each and every moment of your life to grow into your most authentic self. This is your time, your life, your opportunity to grow and be all that you are. Let your heart guide you. Embrace yourself fully and completely. Acknowledge yourself and remain open to your deepest, most pure feelings of love.

Affirmation: I am committed to living this moment with full awareness of my true self.

"Be yourself; everyone else is already taken."
–Oscar Wilde

You must love and honor yourself. There are no mistakes in the grand scheme of the universe. You are unique and special. Your only real responsibility is to grow and become all that you are capable of. Some people will love you and others will not. You cannot be responsible for their decisions, but you must never let their decisions alter your primary responsibility to live your life fully and completely. The world has never been graced with you before, so don't cheat the world out of this opportunity.

**Affirmation: Today I am giving the world my greatest gift--
myself.**

"Hope will never be silent."
–Harvey Milk

Meditation on hope.

Close your eyes and take three deep breaths. Then open your eyes.

Look closely at one section of the mandala. Imagine this single section of the mandala represents who you are today.

Next, allow your focus to shift to the entire mandala. Imagine that the entire mandala represents your entire life.

Notice that your current experience is simply one tiny piece of the much larger tapestry of your life.

If things are not as you would have them right now, don't give up hope.

Your life is much bigger and beautiful than the one tiny section.

See yourself as the larger design of the entire mandala.

You are a beautiful design, made up of many distinct moments.

Affirmation: I am worthy of happiness, unconditional love, and acceptance--just as I am.

"If you're going through hell, keep going."
—Winston Churchill

Never give up. If things are difficult for you now, remember the one constant in life is that things do not remain constant. The pain you are going through now will not be permanent. There may be times when you feel like giving up, but remember, your life is a precious gift. Your story has yet to be told. The world awaits who you will become and the things you will accomplish.

Affirmation: I experience shelter and comfort in the knowledge that my story is still unfolding.

"Love has reasons which reason cannot understand."
–Blaise Pascal

We do not choose our sexual orientation or gender identity. These aspects of ourselves can sometimes feel confusing because who we are and who we love may not fit what others expect of us. Even though your feelings won't always make sense, allow yourself to have the space you need to live your life in the most authentic way possible.

Affirmation: I acknowledge that I don't have all the answers and I embrace myself as I am, knowing that the rest of my story has yet to unfold.

**"We can easily forgive a child who is afraid of the dark;
the real tragedy of life is when adults are afraid of the light."
–Unknown**

Homosexuality is not a choice, but homophobia is.

There is no evidence that anyone has ever been able to change their sexual orientation. It is a fact that sexual orientation is not a matter of choice. However, our dislike and fear of others is certainly a learned behavior. This is another reason why it is important to show compassion as we strive to understand those who are different from us. For as we become better acquainted with each other, the hatred and misinformation will fade away.

Affirmation: Today I will acknowledge myself with love and I will show compassion to those who are not yet able to fully embrace themselves.

**"We are all here to be a service to those who can't be a service
to themselves.
We can give people hope and more reasons for being human."
–Dionne Warwick**

The anatomy of the body is not always congruent with the psychological and emotional sense of gender. Some people do not identify with their biological anatomy. They may identify with another gender or no gender.

To those who are leading human consciousness as we shift in our understanding of gender: we need you at this time in human history. You are here to lead us to deeper understandings of what it means to be human.

Societies learn and grow in ways that are not linear. There will be progress and there will be setbacks. So please stay strong as you live your life authentically and courageously.

Affirmation: Today I embrace my deepest and most authentic sense of gender.

"Do something wonderful, people may imitate it."
–Albert Schweitzer

No matter your gender identity or expression, you are worthy of unconditional love and acceptance.

Starting today, live your life fully and completely. Embrace all that you are. Recognize that your life is a gift. Commit to being the most authentic version of yourself that you can be. As you open yourself more to what it means to truly love and accept yourself, trust that those around you will follow your lead. If they are not quite there yet, embrace them with love. From this place, you can see the potential for love and self-acceptance in others even if they have not yet been able to experience it for themselves. Remember that people cannot give to others what they themselves do not yet have.

Affirmation: I am committed to living an authentic life. I will embrace others with the type of love that always triumphs over fear and hate.

**"Love takes off the masks that we fear we cannot live without
and know we cannot live within."
–James Arthur Baldwin**

The greatest gift we have is our own inner experience. It is from this deep well of feelings, thoughts, and dreams that we become more of who we are. Never allow yourself to think that you don't matter or that your experience of love is not valid.

Affirmation: Today I choose love and I will lead others by embracing them in love.

"We know what we are, but know not what we may be."
—William Shakespeare

The world is better with you in it. There are gifts and talents that only you possess. Allow your deep passions and love to breathe life into all that is you. Tap into your strength and courage to share yourself with the world. All of humanity will benefit when you embrace who you are meant to be.

Affirmation: I embrace the reality of not yet knowing all that I can be, while trusting that each day I am becoming more of who I am meant to be.

**"Whoever has the heart's doors
wide open
can see the sun itself
in every atom."
—Rumi**

Being honest with yourself may not be easy, but hiding what is natural for you can make you feel worse.

You are a shining beacon of love and light. Allow your authentic self to shine. We need you!

Affirmation: Today I embrace myself with love and acceptance.

**"Hope lies in dreams, in imagination,
and in the courage of those who dare to make dreams
into reality."
–Jonas Salk**

Each day, allow yourself to connect to your deepest self. Breathe; sit with your breathing. When your mind drifts, come back to the breathing. Over and over again, allow yourself to feel the stillness of your breathing. It is in this space of stillness that a deeper hope resides. It is a hope that can acknowledge things as they are and can understand that you have the resources to get through whatever challenges come your way.

Affirmation: Today I tap into the strength that lies within me. Even when I do not feel it, I know it exists in the deep stillness within.

"Few are those who see with their own eyes and feel with their own hearts."
–Albert Einstein

Often we are told what to do. There are many forces that tell us what to believe, what to fear, who to love, and how to love. But the best source of information comes from within you. Allow yourself to focus awareness on your heart and mind. Allow your deep information to emerge into awareness. Let it guide and protect you. You have a profound responsibility to bring yourself into the fullness of all that you can be. You are the only one who can do this. So please, take a moment today to honor yourself. And always remember that you are the most important person you will ever meet.

Affirmation: Today I will get to know myself just a little bit more.

"The soul that is within me no man can degrade."
–Frederick Douglass

Take a few moments right now to close your eyes. Take a few deep breaths. Come into contact with the gentle inflow and outflow of your breath. Find this quiet space inside of you and know that it is available for you anytime you need it. This is one portal into the depths of your soul. Remember that this space inside of you cannot be diminished or destroyed by forces outside of you. It is the Sacred within.

Affirmation: The quiet place inside of myself can never be taken away by someone else.

"Love is all around, flowing and ever available. Even in what feels like the worst of times.
If you allow it, love fills you up. It mends the tattered and broken spaces in your spirit.
It makes you feel whole."
−Oprah Winfrey

When you feel down, remember that you are worthy of love just as you are. Others may not yet be able to manifest love for you, but never let that diminish your internal and infinite river of love and self-acceptance. You are a beautiful human being.

Take a few moments right now to close your eyes, take a few deep breaths, and with each inhalation, imagine you are taking in life and goodness. Then as you exhale, imagine that source of deep, powerful love flowing out of you and into the universe.

Affirmation: Infinite love and strength are available to me.

"The most certain way to succeed is always to try just one more time."
–Thomas Edison

You have unrealized potential inside. This part of you is patiently waiting for you to tap into it. Allow yourself time each day to quietly invite it to manifest in your life. The world has never seen you before--and you have gifts that no other person has ever brought forward.

Affirmation: Today I vow to never give up on myself.

"Love consists of this: two solitudes that meet, protect, and greet each other."
–Rainer Maria Rilke

How and when two people find each other is a mystery of the ages. Love is greater than our capacity to control and yet when it happens to us and we are able to connect with another person, we become more fully human. When we are able to journey through life with another person at our side, we rejoice. Love is to be celebrated. Never let your love be diminished.

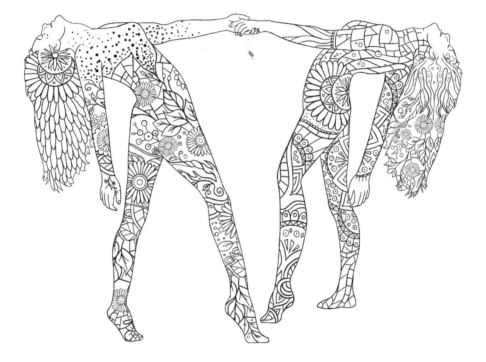

Affirmation: I am an open vessel for love. I give and receive love freely. I do this without conditions.

"Love is composed of a single soul inhabiting two bodies."
–Aristotle

A loving relationship can be the best mirror into your soul. Love expands us beyond our limits. When you open your heart to love another person, you open yourself to grow beyond the limits of your individual self. In this way, love helps us to become greater versions of ourselves.

Affirmation: I am growing because I am a loving human being.

"A small body of determined spirits fired by an unquenchable faith in their mission can alter the course of history."
—Mahatma Gandhi

Be open to whenever you have the opportunity to love another. When you lift up another person in love, you grow and expand what is best in yourself. When you allow your life to be led by love, you will find more love being returned to you.

Affirmation: Today I see myself growing as a person who loves without limits.

"We see the world, not as it is, but as we are."
—Anonymous

One of the best sources of information about yourself is to look at your close relationships. Do you see strife, jealousy, indifference? Or do you see respect, acceptance, and love?

Take a moment today to reflect on a few of your close relationships. Let this information help you learn about your deeper self. Sometimes this information is difficult to take in. But don't judge it; just observe. Then allow this awareness help you create the world you most want for yourself.

Affirmation: Today I am open to seeing myself as I am reflected in my relationships.

"Darkness cannot drive out darkness;
only light can do that.
Hate cannot drive out hate;
only love can do that."
–Martin Luther King Jr.

In the face of inequality and discrimination, we can rise above the pain by loving and respecting one another. No matter how much destruction is wrought by the forces of fear and hatred, they will inevitably crumble when love breaks through. So be strong, and remember that love always conquers hate.

Affirmation: Today I am choosing love over fear. Today I am choosing love over hate.

"To forgive is to set a prisoner free and discover that the prisoner was you."
–Lewis B. Smedes

Forgiveness is one the greatest gifts of healing that you have to offer yourself. Some people think that forgiveness is something that you would do for the benefit of the person who hurt you. But forgiveness is really about letting go of the burden you are carrying. Letting go in forgiveness frees you from having to carry the painful energy from the injury. You become lighter and more free to move forward in life. So for your benefit, think of someone you can forgive and then practice forgiveness as an act of healing yourself.

Affirmation: Today I am going to forgive someone as an act of healing myself.

"We must let go of the life we have planned,
so as to accept the one that is waiting for us."
–Joseph Campbell

When someone comes out to you, remember that they are exactly the same person they were the day before you found out. The only difference now is that you know them better.

When we are afraid, we may reject others; but when we open our hearts with love, we experience a boundless flow of warmth and acceptance. It is through love that we are able to transcend our fears.

Always remember that our human capacity for love and acceptance is ultimately greater than our fears.

Affirmation: Today I will acknowledge my fears and prejudices. Then I will embrace love and acceptance. Fear and hatred will start to fade from my life.

"There is no force more liberating than the knowledge that you are fighting for others."
–Bob Kerrey

Scapegoating others is a false escape from complex problems. Our highest concern is the welfare of others, particularly the most vulnerable among us. When we fight for those who cannot fight for themselves, we expand healing for everyone. So we must always stand up for those who are oppressed. When we honor and lift up others with dignity, particularly those who are different from us, we tap into genuine strength and power.

Affirmation: Today I am fighting for those who cannot fight for themselves.

**"This is the miracle that happens every time to those who really love:
the more they give, the more they possess."
–Rainer Maria Rilke**

If you are feeling down, then go find a stranger and practice doing random acts of kindness. Allow yourself to show compassion; give to another with no expectations. Then, if you still feel down, repeat the process over and over again. Soon you will find that instead of feeling depleted, you are being rejuvenated. This is the greatest gift of the day. So allow yourself to receive it with an open heart.

Affirmation: Today I am open to receiving the gift that comes from giving to others.

"We must accept finite disappointment, but never lose infinite hope."
–Martin Luther King Jr.

Hope is not simply the Pollyanna principle of being glad or positive. While there is tremendous benefit in being able to ground ourselves in a state of gratitude, there is a deeper sense of hope to focus on today. This is the hope of knowing that you have the resources to get through whatever challenges you face. It is a hope that is grounded in the knowledge that you have power deep within yourself. This is a power to push into and through the pain of today in order to create a better world. This opens you to an infinite hope.

Affirmation: Today I am opening myself to the greater power within myself and will use this to help change the world.

**"Love recognizes no barriers.
It jumps hurdles, leaps fences,
penetrates walls to arrive at its destination full of hope."
–Maya Angelou**

There are many forces that attempt to divide us from each other. When we split ourselves internally or from others that we perceive as being different from us, we diminish ourselves. The antidote to splitting is love. Love is a bridge that connects us to each other. It transcends the perceived boundaries between self and other. Love enriches each person as an individual.

**Affirmation: Today I have the courage to push beyond my comfort zones
as I trust in the power of love to guide me.**

**"If we have no peace,
it is because we have forgotten that we belong to each other."
—Mother Teresa**

Meditation on peace.

Close your eyes and take three deep breaths. Then open your eyes.

Look closely at one section of the mandala. Imagine this single section represents you. All of your past, present, and future is represented in that tiny section.

Now allow your focus to shift to the entire mandala. Imagine the entire mandala represents all of life.

Notice that while you may be distinct in many ways, you are also a part of a much larger tapestry.

Take a moment to allow yourself to experience the connection to all that is.

Affirmation: Today I am becoming aware of how connected I am to all of life.

"We may have all come on different ships, but we're in the same boat now."
–Martin Luther King Jr.

No other person has been given the opportunity to live your life. That job rests completely with you. Yet the thing we share in common with each other is that we are unique. This is a powerful bond. We must never allow ourselves to be split from one another due to our differences. Rather, we must come together and be stronger because of those differences. Remember that you are not alone.

Affirmation: Today I commit myself to living my life fully, and in doing so, I am committing to the welfare of all life.

"Where there is love there is life."
–Mahatma Gandhi

Poets, philosophers, artists, and scientists have tried to understand the experience we call "love." Yet all of our language and works of art are mere symbols. Love transcends our capacity to fully capture it.

There may be times when you hear someone say that love can only happen within the limits of a heterosexual relationship. But when the heart is open, we realize that love is much greater than the limits some have tried to impose upon it. Love ultimately transcends all labels and categories that have been created around it.

Work each day to find the courage to surrender to the power of love.

Affirmation: Today my heart will lead me toward a more whole experience of life.

"Love cures people--
both the ones who give it
and the ones who receive it."
–Karl Menninger

If you feel alone and rejected because of who you love or who you are, never give up hope. You are worthy of unconditional love and acceptance just as you are.

When you open yourself to this fact, you can tap into a light within yourself that can never be extinguished by someone else. Your capacity to love yourself and love others is greater than anything that could diminish you.

Affirmation: Today I commit to one thing: I commit to the greatest part of myself. I commit to love.

**"Love and compassion are necessities, not luxuries.
Without them humanity cannot survive."
–Dalai Lama**

Love and compassion are essential nutrients for the human soul. Ironically, the more we give them away, the more we find of them inside ourselves. They become infinite sources of life within. Each one of us has a unique flavor of love and compassion. So today, focus on ways to bring your love and compassion into the world. Let them manifest in new and unplanned ways. Give them away freely and you'll be all the more filled with them.

Affirmation: Today I commit to being a master philanthropist of love.

"Love tells us that we have connected to our true purpose."
—Deepak Chopra

Love is a powerful source of information that can guide your life. Some people may try to tell you that your love is bad, sinful, or not good enough. Whenever you encounter these people, simply embrace them with compassion. It may be that they have not yet had the courage to open themselves to love. Love does not take directions, nor does it follow the orders of leaders and religions. It transcends and is greater than all of these external human attempts to control it.

**Affirmation: Today I acknowledge the deep source of love within.
I feel gratitude because I am guided by love.**

**"Let yourself be silently drawn by the strange pull of what you really love.
It will not lead you astray."
—Rumi**

It's important to honor love as it manifests in your life. Love is not about possessing someone or diminishing them. Love is something that is given freely and unconditionally. When you love in this way, you may experience challenges, rejection, and disapproval, but love remains a steady beacon that can lead you to a more expanded and authentic life. So trust the wisdom of this deeper part of yourself.

Affirmation: I trust love.

**"Be soft. Do not let the world make you hard.
Do not let the pain make you hate.
Do not let the bitterness steal your sweetness.
Take pride that even though the rest of the world
may disagree,
you still believe it to be a beautiful place."
–Iain S. Thomas**

Life does not come with a guarantee that it will be easy. Often people face very real discrimination, injustice, and hatred because of who they love. This might cause a person to turn their heart cold and close off from love. However, when we keep our hearts open in the face of the pain, we can experience a rich and beautiful place where hate does not win. Love truly does transform hate.

Affirmation: I am choosing to let go of fear and embrace love.

"Love is patient, love is kind. It does not envy, it does not boast, it is not proud. It does not dishonor others, it is not self-seeking, it is not easily angered, it keeps no record of wrongs. Love does not delight in evil but rejoices with the truth. It always protects, always trusts, always hopes, always perseveres. Love never fails."
1 Corinthians 13:4–8 NIV

Sometimes you may not feel much love in your life. It may be so far in the background that it becomes almost imperceptible. And there may be times when it seems that it is nowhere to be found--but know that it is always present. Other people, institutions, religions, and nations will come and go, but love will remain. Love will never fail you.

You have a choice in each and every moment of life. So choose the path of love.

Affirmation: Today, and every day, I choose love.

ABOUT THE AUTHORS

Dr. Ronald Holt is a board-certified psychiatrist and a motivational speaker, author, and facilitator, who resides in San Francisco, California. He is passionate about issues relevant to lesbian, gay, bisexual, and transgender (LGBT) communities and is a leader in the LGBT happiness and mental health world.

He travels to schools, universities, hospitals and corporations where he provides lectures and experiential learning on issues related to LGBT health and well-being. The information he presents is useful to all people as we work to create a better world for everyone.

Dr. Holt has written the international bestselling book *PRIDE: You Can't Heal If You're Hiding from Yourself.* www.amazon.com/dp/B01MXXW0ZF.

You can find out more about Dr. Holt by going to his website: www.DrRonHolt.com or www.DrRonHolt.info

Dr. William Huggett is a psychoanalyst and board-certified psychiatrist. He has a private practice where he focuses on helping individuals access the wealth of information and resources that exist within themselves. His goal is to help individuals be better equipped to live their lives aligned with their most authentic self. He helps clients develop their own tools including meditation, relaxation training, diet, physical exercise, and mindfulness techniques.

You can find out more about Dr. Huggett by visiting his website, www.williamhuggett.com.

Made in the USA
Coppell, TX
15 July 2020